# Girls'

# HOCKEY

by Chris Peters

GIRLS'

SportsZone

Published by ABDO Publishing Company, PO Box 398166, Minneapolis, MN 55439. Copyright © 2014 by Abdo Consulting Group, Inc. International copyrights reserved in all countries. No part of this book may be reproduced in any form without written permission from the publisher. SportsZone™ is a trademark and logo of ABDO Publishing Company.

Printed in the United States of America,
North Mankato, Minnesota

052013
092013

Editor: Chrös McDougall
Series Designer: Marie Tupy

**Photo Credits:** Shutterstock Images, cover, 1; Josh Holmberg/Icon SMI, 5, 27; Bob Frid/Icon SMI, 6, 13; David Stluka/AP Images, 8, 11, 17; Chris O'Meara/AP Images, 14; Gene J. Puskar/AP Images, 19; Newspix/Icon SMI, 21; Zuma Press/Icon SMI, 23; Bruce Bennett/Getty Images, 25; Cal Sport Media/AP Images, 29; Toby Talbot/AP Images, 31; Gene J. Puskar/AP Images, 33; The Star Tribune/Marlin Levison/AP Images, 35; Cris Bouroncle/AFP/Getty Images, 37; Julie Jacobson/AP Images, 39; The Canadian Press/Adrian Wyld/AP Images, 41, 42; Red Line Editorial, 44

Library of Congress Control Number: 2013932516

**Cataloging-in-Publication Data**

Peters, Chris.
 Girls' hockey / Chris Peters.
   p. cm. -- (Girls' sportszone )
 ISBN 978-1-61783-987-0  (lib. bdg.)
 Includes bibliographical references and index.
 1. Hockey for girls--Juvenile literature.   I. Title.
 796.962--dc23

                                              2013932516

**GIRLS' SportsZone**

Table of Contents

# chapter 1

# Skating with Hilary Knight

Hilary Knight was only 20 years old when she heard the announcement. She had been selected to the US women's hockey team that would compete in the 2010 Olympic Winter Games in Vancouver. She was the youngest member of Team USA. But the Hanover, New Hampshire, native made her presence known. She scored a goal and had eight points in five Olympic games. Her efforts helped Team USA win the silver medal.

That tournament put Knight on the map. She has been one of Team USA's go-to scorers ever since. In fact, she is becoming one of the best players in the world. A lot of that has to do with her skating abilities.

Team USA's Hilary Knight skates toward the action during a game prior to the 2010 Olympic Winter Games.

Knight boasts tremendous speed and footwork. This allows her to get around the other team's defense. The former University of Wisconsin player often wins races to a loose puck. Plus she is strong enough on her skates that she rarely gets the puck taken away from her. Knight is a great puck handler and has a great shot. But without her strong skating, she probably would not score as many goals as she does.

One example of Knight's great speed came at the 2012 Women's World Championship in Burlington, Vermont. Team USA was playing against Russia in front of the home fans. Knight and her teammates put on quite

Hilary Knight (21) prepares to drive past a Canada player during the 2010 Olympic gold-medal game.

a show. After scoring earlier on in the game on a pretty stickhandling display, Knight showed off her explosive skating.

Team USA was starting to pull away from Russia with a 4–0 lead in the third period. It would have been understandable if the Americans started easing up a bit. But Knight was not about to slow down.

With the puck way back in Team USA's zone, Knight started skating hard up the ice to put herself in a good position to catch a pass. She got up to the Russian blue line so quickly, the defenders did not even see her. Knight looked around to see where her teammates were. Then she cut to the middle of the ice.

Defenseman Megan Bozek saw Knight. Bozek sent a long pass that hit her teammate in stride. As soon as Knight got the puck, she turned on the jets. The Russian defenders had no chance of catching her. Knight skated

## AMANDA KESSEL

Amanda Kessel comes from a strong hockey family. Her brother Phil Kessel plays for the Toronto Maple Leafs. He is one of the best scorers in the National Hockey League (NHL). Amanda is also one of the fastest skaters and best scorers in the game. In 2013 she won the Patty Kazmaier Award as the best player in women's college hockey. "She's going to be one of the best players in the world," said Noora Räty, Kessel's University of Minnesota teammate and Team Finland superstar goalie. "She's the fastest player I've ever seen."

in on a breakaway and fired the puck right over the goalie's shoulder to give Team USA a 5–0 lead. The US team went on to win that game 9–0.

By using her quick feet, Knight was able to catch the defensemen by surprise. They were too slow to react and could not catch up. As a result, Knight had a clear path to the net and scored an easy goal.

## It Starts with Skating

In hockey, it all starts with skating. Skating is the most important skill to learn and get better at. Skating affects just about every aspect of hockey.

Hilary Knight, playing for the University of Wisconsin, brings the puck up the ice during a 2011 game.

Great skating—and with it great speed—often sets apart the good players from the great players.

Skating is fundamental to playing hockey. You can't play without being able to skate. That is why most coaches recommend taking time to learn how to skate well before playing one period of hockey. Even after a player knows *how* to skate, it is important that she always continues to work on getting better. The best hockey players never stop practicing their skating skills.

Being a good skater takes a lot of balance and coordination. Being balanced is a big key for hockey. Trying to stand up on the thin skate blades can seem a little hard at first. That is what practice is for. Once a player can stand up and move around, she can work on turning, footwork, and especially speed.

## RACING FOR A PUCK

**Hockey is a superfast game. It almost seems like everything is a race. Some of the toughest races are the ones for a loose puck. Having the puck is the only way to score goals, so everyone wants to control it. When there is a chance to get the puck, everyone seems to race a little faster. This is one area of the game where skating plays the most important part. The first key is quickly getting to the puck. Then holding on to it requires good body positioning. To keep control of the puck, the winner of the race has to keep her head up and use her body to protect the puck from defenders to make sure all that hard work to get there pays off.**

# Quick Tip: Skating Backward

Skating forward seems hard enough, but skating backward is even tougher. The best way to generate some balance and speed is with a deep knee bend, almost like sitting in a chair. Bending the knees creates more balance and also allows the skater to generate more power. With more power comes more speed and the ability to keep up with the opposing player who is skating forward. In practice, work on skating backward and really bending your knees. That will help you be more prepared to skate backward in a game.

The speed of hockey makes it important to develop quickness in skating. That quickness can help players get around the defense, win races for loose pucks, and make it tougher for the other team to get the puck.

Skating plays a role in almost every skill in hockey. Being a good skater can instantly make a player more effective at skills such as stickhandling, shooting, or passing.

Stickhandling is about speed and control. A player who is balanced on her skates is faster and more in control. Without this balance, a player will have a difficult time generating speed. That makes it easier for an opposing player to steal the puck.

When it comes to shooting pucks, most of the power a player can put behind a shot comes from the legs. So a player with good balance will be able to shoot the puck harder and more accurately. The same is true for passing. A player who is good on her skates is going to make better passes.

Skating plays such an important role in trying to score goals. However, it is just as important in preventing them. Defensemen spend a lot of their time skating backward. That is another area where balance comes into play. Additionally, forwards have to be good teammates and help out in the defensive zone by being good back-checkers.

Everything happens very fast on the ice, so being able to read where the puck is going and react quickly to it will help.

Wisconsin Badgers forward Hilary Knight handles the puck against Boston University during a 2011 game.

Agosta's stick got there first. Agosta quickly pivoted on her skates and took one look at the net. US players surrounded her. Yet Agosta was able to get a quick wrist shot up and over the sprawled-out Schaus. The puck fluttered inside the left post and into the net. The game was tied.

"We just kept battling, I don't even know how it happened, but the puck came out and I just shot it and it ended up going in the net," Agosta said before the overtime period.

Canada went on to win the game in overtime. That gave Canada its tenth world championship in 14 tries. Team USA had won the previous three world titles. It looked as if the United States would win a fourth

Meghan Agosta (2) shoots against Switzerland during the 2010 Olympic Winter Games in Vancouver.

before Agosta's timely goal. But the former Mercyhurst College star kept Canada alive against its archrival.

Agosta is no stranger to big goals. She scored a record nine times in the 2010 Olympic Winter Games in Vancouver. The Ruthven, Ontario, native seems to know how to be in the right place at the right time. And when she's there, she makes it count with a good, hard shot.

So how does Agosta score so much? Part of it is good instincts, but the biggest reason is her amazing wrist shot.

# Winning with a Wrist Shot

The wrist shot is widely considered the most effective shot in hockey. It is easily the most accurate shot and typically the easiest to get off. The wrist shot is also fairly easy to learn. And with practice, it's not all that hard to perfect.

A good, hard wrist shot is probably the best shot for scoring goals. That is because it is the easiest to control. The puck stays on the blade of the stick longer when taking a wrist shot. And with a good follow-through, a player can direct it to go wherever she wants.

The wrist shot is not just for scoring goals either. It can come in handy for defenders as well. When playing in the defensive zone, sometimes there is no one open for a pass. When that's the case, clearing the puck from the defensive zone is the next best option to avoid the pressure. A good wrist shot raises the puck off the ice. That makes it tough for the opposing players to keep the puck in the zone. It might lead to icing, but a good clearance is better than turning the puck over to the other team.

## BRIANNA DECKER

Brianna Decker won the Patty Kazmaier Award in 2012. That award is given each year to the best women's college hockey player. Decker scored 37 goals for the University of Wisconsin that season to lead the nation. Many of them came off her deadly wrist shot. She developed a great wrist shot through repetition. Decker's brother, Ben Decker, also plays hockey. He said the duo spends a lot of their free time at home practicing their shots. "When we're home, we're always bored," Ben said. "We probably shoot 300 pucks each time we're down there." Repetition like that, even if it's only to kill time while bored, helps perfect the skill.

Brianna Decker of Wisconsin shoots during a 2010 game against the Minnesota State Mavericks.

## Quick Tip: The Weight Transfer

One of the lesser known but perhaps most important traits of the wrist shot is the weight transfer. Much of the shot's power is generated through shifting one's weight from the back leg to the front. The most powerful wrist shots will start with the puck behind the player. While sweeping the puck forward, the player's weight and balance shifts. As the player shifts, the puck will move from the heel of the stick to toe naturally. Staying balanced with a good wide stance and hands properly positioned on the stick will lead to a much harder shot.

There are four parts to a good wrist shot. They are hand positioning, transferring weight from the back leg to the front, keeping an eye on where the puck should go, and a quick flick of the wrists. When all of that is put together, the shot will be powerful and more accurate. The shot will also get away from the stick more quickly.

Perfecting the technique of a good wrist shot takes time. Repetition is the best way to improve the wrist shot. With more practice, the shot becomes more accurate, quicker on the release, and also much faster.

Players with a good, accurate wrist shot are very difficult to defend. A good wrist shot can catch goalies and defensemen off guard because of how quick it can come off the stick. Sometimes all it takes is a subtle flick of the wrists and the puck is in the back of the net.

Maria Rooth of Sweden shoots and scores the game-winning goal against Team USA in the 2006 Olympic semifinals.

# 3

# Stickhandling with the Lamoureux Twins

Jean-Pierre and Linda Lamoureux have six children. Hockey was seemingly in their blood. The four oldest sons were all hockey stars. Two played college hockey at the University of North Dakota. One played college hockey at the Air Force Academy. The biggest hockey stars in the family, though, are the youngest sisters, twins Jocelyne and Monique Lamoureux.

Jocelyne and Monique honed their immense hockey skills as kids on a frozen stream in Grand Forks, North Dakota. Today, they are two of the most exciting women's hockey players because of their creativity when they stickhandle.

Jocelyne Lamoureux skates up the rink with the puck against Russia during the 2011 World Championships.

## TIPPING SHOTS

Jocelyne Lamoureux scored the big goal at the Olympic Winter Games. However, Monique Lamoureux is a pretty gifted scorer herself. She stood out during a preliminary-round game against Canada at the 2012 Women's World Championship. Monique scored three times as Team USA went on to blow out its biggest rival by a score of 9–2. Stickhandling also requires good hand-eye coordination. That hand-eye coordination also comes in handy in deflecting the puck. Two of Monique's goals in that hat trick came after she tipped the puck with her stick from someone else's shot. Deflecting the puck is another important stick skill that can help lead to goals.

The twin sisters entered the spotlight in 2008 when they joined the University of Minnesota hockey team. Both were stars. They did not feel at home, though. Both sisters transferred to North Dakota after one year. They helped make North Dakota a top team in women's hockey during their time there. They also made their mark with Team USA.

Both sisters were named to the 2010 US Olympic hockey team. And they put on a show for much of the tournament in Vancouver. It was Jocelyne, however, who scored an amazing goal in a preliminary-round game against China.

Team USA was already up 7-0 late in the second period. Then Jocelyne grabbed a loose puck just inside the blue line in the offensive zone. She had one defenseman to beat. But she was coming down the left side of the ice. That was not ideal for the right-handed shooter. She would not have been able to get a good enough shot from the left side with a defenseman between her and the goal.

So she did not try. Instead, Jocelyne faked like she was going to cut to the middle. As the defenseman closed in, Jocelyne did something quite unexpected, catching everyone in the arena by surprise, especially the China defender.

With amazing quickness and control, Jocelyne used great stick control and skating to deke the defenseman. While skating toward the

Monique Lamoureux skates with the puck against Canada during the 2013 World Championships.

## HONING CREATIVITY

The Lamoureux twins grew up in a hockey-loving family. Jocelyne and Monique spent hours and hours with their older brothers playing hockey on the frozen stream near their house. Those pick-up games are a big reason the twins became such good puck handlers. That is because they were just having fun. Stickhandling is something that takes practice, but sometimes the best practice is just trying something new with friends. It's one of the fun elements of the game, and players get to use their imagination to create new ways to get around defenders.

defenseman, Jocelyne flicked the puck back to her right and through her legs. The puck slid out to her left. So Jocelyne changed direction on the spot and followed the puck left. Never losing control of the puck, she skated around the defenseman and slipped a point-blank shot right between the goalie's legs.

Even legendary play-by-play announcer Mike "Doc" Emrick was stunned. "Oh, my," he exclaimed.

Two-time US Olympian A. J. Mleczko was the color commentator. After describing the goal on replay to the television audience, she said, "That's a move she probably learned playing on that pond in North Dakota. That is a highlight goal."

Because of her terrific stickhandling, Jocelyne was able to turn nothing into something. Most players would just try to shoot through or around the defender. Instead, Jocelyne used her creativity to create a better scoring opportunity.

## Stickhandling to Success

As Jocelyne Lamoureux showed, good stickhandling can help create goals and scoring opportunities. There are a variety of moves or dekes a player can make to give her some time and space.

Stickhandling is more than just making creative moves though. It is all about carrying the puck effectively.

Puck handling takes some concentration. A player has to be able to see where she is going. She has to be able to handle the puck while keeping her head up. Not being able to look at the puck can be challenging, but it is

Jocelyne Lamoureux of Team USA celebrates after scoring against China during the 2010 Olympic Winter Games.

## Quick Tip: Off-ice Practice

The great thing about stick handling is that it doesn't require ice to practice. All that is required is a hard surface, a stick, and a golf ball. Wait. A golf ball? It might sound silly, but a golf ball can be difficult to control, which makes it perfect for stickhandling. Moving your hands as though you're handling a puck, you can easily feel the golf ball through the stick, so it's a good way to practice keeping your head up. The better you get, the faster you'll be able to go and the less you'll have to look down.

crucial to success. It allows the player to survey the area and see if she has open teammates or a chance for a shot on net.

In hockey, it is pretty simple. The team that possesses the puck most effectively is usually going to be the team that wins. Passing is important, too. But handling the puck is a major key of puck possession. If a player can't handle the puck, she is more likely to turn the puck over to the other team.

The advanced players are the ones who can make the moves like Jocelyne Lamoureux did at the Olympic Winter Games. There are a variety of ways to beat a defender, but the players that can do it with crafty stickhandling usually end up on the highlight films.

Monique Lamoureux controls the puck during an exhibition game before the 2010 Olympic Winter Games.

# 4

# Passing with Amanda Kessel

In 2012–13 Amanda Kessel and her University of Minnesota teammates did the incredible. The Golden Gophers played 41 games. They won all 41. No team had ever gone undefeated in Division I college women's hockey. And in doing so, they won a second consecutive national title. At the center of the run was Kessel. She was named that season's Patty Kazmaier Award winner as the best player in women's college hockey.

That season confirmed Kessel was one of the brightest young stars in women's hockey. She is a terrific goal scorer. But what a lot of people forget is that she might be an even better passer.

Amanda Kessel (8) celebrates with University of Minnesota teammate
Hannah Brandt (22) during the 2013 college championship game.

## THE SAUCER PASS

The saucer pass is one of the toughest skills in hockey to perfect. This pass is particularly effective when there is an obstacle, such as a defenseman's stick or a player sliding on the ice, in between the passer and her target. A saucer pass lifts the puck about 8 to 10 inches (20–25 cm) off the ice. Then the puck spins in the air like a Frisbee so that it lands flat on its side when it reaches the receiver. If the puck lands on its edge it could bounce and be harder to receive. It's usually a last resort, but it can be very effective.

With a good combination of speed, vision, and creativity, Kessel is a great teammate because she is unselfish with the puck. Most goal scorers want the puck on their sticks all the time. Kessel knows that sometimes a teammate will have a better shot.

That attitude showed at the 2012 Women's World Championships, when Kessel was still in college. She collected seven assists in five games. Her biggest assist came in the gold-medal game.

Team USA was trailing Canada 1–0 in the first period. Kessel found herself with some space coming out of the left corner. She coolly took a look around to see what was going on in front of the net. Two teammates were there, but both were well covered.

Kessel then began skating toward the middle of the ice. She faked like she was about to shoot. One of the Canadian defenders bit and started charging at Kessel. As the defender started skating toward her, Kessel kept her eyes on the front of the net. She was watching to see if she had any kind of opening to find a teammate close to the net.

US forward Kendall Coyne was battling for position in front but was still covered well by a Canadian defender. Yet for just a split second she got a good enough position to get the stick on the puck. As soon as Coyne freed herself up, Kessel wired a hard pass toward the net. It hit Coyne right on the tape of her stick and slid into the net. The game was tied.

If Kessel had tried to shoot, she probably would have had the shot blocked by one of the four players in front of the net. Instead she had the patience to make the right decision.

Team USA's Amanda Kessel (28) races down the ice during semifinals of the 2012 World Championships.

Coyne did a great job to get herself open, but Kessel timed her pass perfectly. If she had passed too early or too late, Coyne would have had a harder time getting her stick on the puck. That little bit of patience allowed Kessel to see the opening, and she put the puck in the perfect spot.

## The Positives of Passing

Like all team sports, hockey requires teamwork for success. Passing is the ultimate teamwork play because it gets everyone involved.

Similar to stickhandling, passing is all about one team maintaining possession of the puck. There are times when it is smart to take on a defender one-on-one. However, the safest play when under pressure is usually to

### HAYLEY WICKENHEISER

Hayley Wickenheiser might be the greatest player ever to play the women's game. She appeared in the first four Olympic women's hockey tournaments (1998, 2002, 2006, 2010) for Canada. Wickenheiser was once one of the best goal scorers in the world. Later she became one of the best set-up women. Wickenheiser had 12 assists in the 2006 Winter Games and nine more in 2010. It makes sense that a good goal scorer can become a good passer. The thought process is very similar. In shooting, a player has to identify where the best place to put a shot is. In passing the player has to identify which teammate is open. Wickenheiser also represented Canada as an Olympic softball player in 2000.

pass to an open teammate. That teammate might be in a better position to score a goal or make something else happen.

A good passing team is much more difficult to defend than a team full of players trying to stickhandle around everyone. Continually moving the

Canada's Hayley Wickenheiser skates up the ice during the 2010 Olympic Winter Games in Vancouver.

# Quick Tip: Improving Accuracy

Good passing starts with accuracy. The keys to making an accurate pass include keeping your head up and getting eyes on your intended target. Once you have identified a target, you can improve your accuracy with a good follow-through. On the follow-through, the front of your stick blade should be facing the intended target. This is tougher to practice on your own, but taping a target on a garage door or an overturned bench could be a good way to work on passing.

puck from player to player forces the defense to spread out. That creates openings to generate offense. Then a well placed pass can find a teammate who is in good position to score.

Passing requires good awareness and vision. A player has to know where all of her teammates are. She also has to figure out which one is the best option to pass to. Good stickhandling might buy the passer some time to find the right option, but the decision usually has to be made quickly to make the best pass.

Passing is important in all zones of the ice. In the defensive zone, it is usually best to find an open teammate who is able to get the puck out of the zone. Most teams utilize a play called a breakout to get the puck out of the zone. The most successful breakouts use a lot of puck movement and make it tougher for the attacking team to keep the puck in the zone.

The other element of passing is receiving the puck. Catching a pass is just as important as delivering one. Players who can catch passes in stride will be able to maintain their speed. It takes focus to receive the pass and soft hands to hold on to it. Catching a pass cleanly can be the difference between a goal and a turnover.

Amanda Kessel advances the puck against Wisconsin during the 2012 college championship game.

# chapter 5

# Goaltending with Jessie Vetter

Jessie Vetter must have a really big trophy case in her house. After all, she has won championships at pretty much every level she's played. And since she's a goalie, she also gets a lot of credit when her teams win.

Through 2013, Vetter won three college national championships with the University of Wisconsin, four gold medals at the Women's World Championship, and an Olympic silver medal. She was also the Patty Kazmaier Award winner as the best player in women's college hockey. So it looks like she knows what she's doing between the pipes.

One of Vetter's best performances came at the 2011 Women's World Championship in Zurich, Switzerland. Team USA cruised through the

Team USA goalie Jessie Vetter controls a puck against Canada during the 2010 Olympic gold-medal game.

## TYPES OF SAVES

There are many saves a goalie can make on a shot and a variety of ways to make them. The basics include the glove save. That is when a goalie catches the puck in her catching glove on higher shots. The stick save is one when the goalie uses her stick to steer the puck away from the net. Stick saves are used mostly on shots that are low to the ice. A blocker save is one where the goalie raises her blocker glove to steer the puck away when the puck is too high for her stick. Then there's the kick save. This is when the goalie kicks out her leg pads to stop shots low to the ground.

preliminary round undefeated. That set up a date with Canada in the gold-medal game.

The game was tied at 2–2 late in the third period. Team USA needed a couple of big stops from Vetter to keep their gold-medal dreams alive.

Young Canada star Marie-Philip Poulin-Nadeau took a shot on goal with just more than two minutes to play in regulation. Vetter made a nice blocker save. She made it look easy, but it probably wasn't. The puck soon left the US zone. Within moments, though, the Canadians forced a turnover and were coming right back 2-on-1.

Vetter had to snap back to attention. Poulin-Nadeau and Sarah Vaillancourt came barreling in on Vetter and defenseman Caitlin Cahow. Poulin-Nadeau fired a shot. It caught a piece of Cahow on the way. That caused the shot to slow its pace, leaving Vetter in a bad position with Poulin-Nadeau right in front.

The puck skidded toward Vetter. The US goalie calmly but quickly shifted her pads. She was able to get in front of Poulin-Nadeau's second-chance shot. Vetter made the stop right in front, but the rebound remained free. Vaillancourt was charging hard for the loose puck. Vetter had to

Jessie Vetter (31) guards the net against Canada during the 2012 Olympic gold-medal game against Canada.

sprawl back to protect the open net. With a little help from Cahow to clear the puck away, Vaillancourt was denied.

The game remained tied. Hilary Knight later scored the game-winner in overtime to give Team USA the gold medal. It was a huge victory for the Americans. They were looking for revenge after losing to Canada at the 2010 Olympic Winter Games.

On that crucial play, Vetter showed incredible quickness. That is a trait all goaltenders need to be successful.

## SHANNON SZABADOS

Shannon Szabados started in goal for Canada at the 2010 Olympic Winter Games. Her performance won her praise from even her biggest rivals. Szabados made 28 saves to shut out Team USA in the gold-medal game. She was also named to the all-tournament team. "I have to take my hat off to Shannon Szabados because she played unbelievable," said Team USA's Caitlin Cahow after the gold-medal game. "Some of the saves she made I already had my arms in the air but she came up with the puck." Szabados is also notable because she spent most of her hockey career playing against boys. She even played Canadian Junior A hockey in a boys' league.

## Quickness Between the Pipes

The goaltender is the last line of defense for every team. The big pads goalies wear certainly help in stopping shots. But there is a lot of athleticism involved in goaltending. Goalies need to be able to move around quickly on their skates. Plus they need to be able to jump right back into position if a save results in a rebound.

"There's no position in sports more than playing goal where you have as large an impact on the end result," said Mitch Korn, the goalie coach for the NHL's Nashville Predators.

Though it may not seem like it, there are actually 24 square feet (2.23 square meters) of net for a goalie to cover. No player is big enough to cover

Canada goalie Shannon Szabados makes a save against Finland during the 2013 World Championships.

that kind of space just standing still. A goalie's quickness and reflexes help make up for that lack of size.

Also, with those big pads on, goalies commonly give up rebounds. So a quick recovery from the first save helps the goalie make the save on the second or third chance off rebounds. Vetter showed this ability in the 2011 World Championships title game.

Team USA goalie Jessie Vetter (31) makes a save against Canada's Hayley Wickenheiser (22) during the 2013 World Championships.

# Quick Tip: The Mental Edge

Finland native Noora Räty has become one of the game's great goaltenders. She started playing on Finland's national team when she was 15 years old. She later starred for the University of Minnesota's women's hockey team through 2013. Räty knows goalies need to be more than just quick. "I've seen so many goalies that have just tremendous skills but their mental side is not that good. So you definitely have to have both." Coaches often stress pregame preparation. One tip some goalies have is creating a pregame routine. Sometimes that includes visualizing plays to come. This helps goalies prepare for the upcoming game.

A lot of that quickness comes naturally, through reflexes, hand-eye coordination, and flexibility. However, there are plenty of drills available to help improve that quickness, too.

It is also important to think quickly. Goalies have to read the entire play in front of them. Keeping focused and alert helps goalies make quicker reactions.

According to Korn, reading the play will help the goaltender properly position herself. It also helps her determine what kind of save she'll have to make. If the goalie reads the play wrong, it might not matter how quick her reflexes are in the end. So a sharp mind is just as important as quick reflexes.

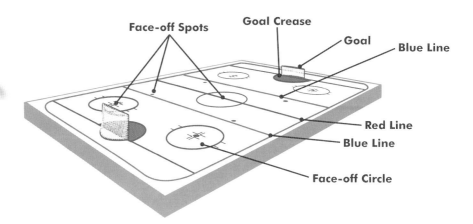

Face-off Spots · Goal Crease · Goal · Blue Line · Red Line · Blue Line · Face-off Circle

## blue lines

The two lines that separate the neutral zone from the offensive and defensive zones

## crease

An area in front of each goal. Attacking players cannot enter the crease before the puck.

## defensive zone

The end of the ice from the blue line to the wall that includes the goal a team has to protect.

## neutral zone

The area in the middle of the ice between the two blue lines.

## offensive zone

The end of the ice from the blue line to the wall that includes the goal a team is trying to score on.

## red line

The center line on a hockey rink.

**assist**

A pass that directly leads to a goal. A maximum of two players can be credited with an assist on any goal.

**back-checkers**

Forwards who are skating back into their defensive zone trying to break up the opposing team's offensive play.

**breakaway**

When an offensive player gets the puck and has no defensive players between her and the goaltender.

**breakout**

When a team takes possession of the puck and moves out of its defensive zone.

**deke**

A move made by a puck handler to get around an opponent.

**face-off**

A play in which the referee drops the puck between one player from each team to start or restart action in a game.

**hat trick**

When a player scores three goals, it is a hockey tradition that fans throw their hats on the ice.

**icing**

A violation that occurs when both teams have an equal number of players on the ice and one team shoots the puck from behind the center red line over the opponent's goal line (but not into the goal).

**rebound**

When a goalie makes a save but the puck remains in play.

**stickhandling**

The act of using the stick to possess the puck. This is also known as puck handling.

**turnover**

When one team loses possession of the puck to the other team.

## Selected Bibliography

Clark, Zac. "What Were You Thinking?" *USA Hockey Magazine.* USA Hockey Magazine. n.d. Web. 22 April 2013.

Huth, Vince. "One Last Go-around." *The Daily Cardinal.* Madison.com. 10 Oct. 2012. Web. 22 April 2013.

King, Katie. "Driveway Drills." *USAHockeyMagazine.com.* USA Hockey Magazine. n.d. Web. 22 April 2013.

Smith, Gary. "House of Hockey." *SI Vault.* Time Inc. 1 Feb. 2010. Web. 22 April 2013.

Thompson, Harry. "The Journey's End: Women Win Silver at 2010 Winter Olympics." *USA Hockey Magazine.* USA Hockey Magazine. April 2010. Web. 22 April 2013.

## Further Readings

Bartsiokas, Tom, and Corey Long. *Angela James: The First Superstar of Women's Hockey.* Toronto, ON: Sumach Press, 2012.

Ruggiero, Angela. *Breaking the Ice.* Plymouth, MA: Drummond Publishing Group, 2005.

Simac, Kimberly Jo. *Girls Play Hockey Too!* Eagle River, WI: Great Northern Adventure Co., Inc., 2007.

Tarcy, Brian, and Tricia Dunn and Katie King. *Gold Medal Ice Hockey for Women and Girls.* Worcester, MA: Chandler House Press, 1999.

Wilson, Stacy. *The Hockey Book for Girls.* Toronto, ON: Kids Can Press, 2000.

# Web Links

To learn more about hockey, visit ABDO Publishing Company online at **www.abdopublishing.com**. Web sites about hockey are featured on our Book Links page. These links are routinely monitored and updated to provide the most current information available.

# Places to Visit

### Hockey Hall of Fame
Brookfield Place
30 Yonge Street
Toronto, ON M5E 1X8, Canada
(416) 360-7765
www.hhof.com

This hall of fame celebrates the history of hockey and its greatest players and contributors through memorabilia and other interactive exhibits. Cammi Granato of the United States and Angela James of Canada were the first female players inducted into the Hockey Hall of Fame in 2010. The Hall is located in downtown Toronto, not far from the Maple Leafs' home arena.

### US Hockey Hall of Fame
801 Hat Trick Avenue
Eveleth, MN 55734
(800) 443-7825
www.ushockeyhall.com

Located in northern Minnesota, this hall of fame and museum celebrates the history of US hockey through various exhibits. There is an entire exhibit dedicated to women's hockey, documenting its history and celebrating the US women's national teams of years past. Both the 1998 US Olympic women's team and Cammi Granato are inductees.

# Index

## ABOUT THE AUTHOR

Chris Peters is a freelance writer based in North Liberty, Iowa. The Chicago native is a contributing writer for CBSSports.com and *USA Hockey Magazine* and is the editor of the United States of Hockey blog. Peters has also written a book about the Stanley Cup Finals. He is a former public relations coordinator with USA Hockey. Peters lives with his wife and son.